Adjectives

Tasty!

Scary!

Frightening!

written by Ann Heinrichs

illustrated by Dan McGeehan and David Moore

The Child's World

Published by The Child's World®
1980 Lookout Drive • Mankato, MN 56003-1705
800-599-READ • www.childsworld.com

ACKNOWLEDGMENTS
The Child's World®: Mary Berendes, Publishing Director
The Design Lab: Design and page production
Red Line Editorial: Editorial direction

LIBRARY OF CONGRESS CATALOGING-IN-PUBLICATION DATA
Heinrichs, Ann.
 Adjectives / by Ann Heinrichs ; illustrated by Dan McGeehan and
David Moore.
     p. cm.
 Includes bibliographical references and index.
 ISBN 978-1-60253-425-4 (library bound : alk. paper)
 1. English language—Adjective—Juvenile literature. I. McGeehan,
Dan, ill. II. Moore, David, ill. III. Title.
 PE1241.H373 2010
 428.2—dc22   2010011445

Printed in the United States of America in Mankato, Minnesota.
July 2010
F11538

ABOUT THE AUTHOR

Ann Heinrichs was lucky. Every year from
grade three through grade eight, she had a
big, fat grammar textbook and a grammar
workbook. She feels that this prepared her
for life. She is now the author of more than
100 books for children and young adults.
She has also enjoyed successful careers as
a children's book editor and an advertising
copywriter. Ann grew up in Fort Smith,
Arkansas, and lives in Chicago, Illinois.

ABOUT THE ILLUSTRATORS

Dan McGeehan spent his younger years
as an actor, author, playwright, cartoonist,
editor, and even as a casket maker. Now he
spends his days drawing little monsters!

David Moore is an illustration instructor
at a university who loves painting and
flying airplanes. Watching his youngest
daughter draw inspires David to illustrate
children's books.

I am fast!

TABLE OF CONTENTS

What Is an Adjective?

noisy

squeaky

longest

sunny

Do you have a noisy dog on your block? Is your desk squeaky? What is the longest book you've ever read? What do you like to do on a sunny day?

All the colored words above are **adjectives**. You can use adjectives to describe just about everything—people and things, activities, feelings, ideas, and more!

Many adjectives answer the question "what kind?"

What kind of cat is that?

It is a Siamese cat.

Adjectives might show number, color, size, or shape.

Ten monsters ate the cake.

Adjectives can tell what something is made of or how it feels.

Sophie sat in a soft chair.

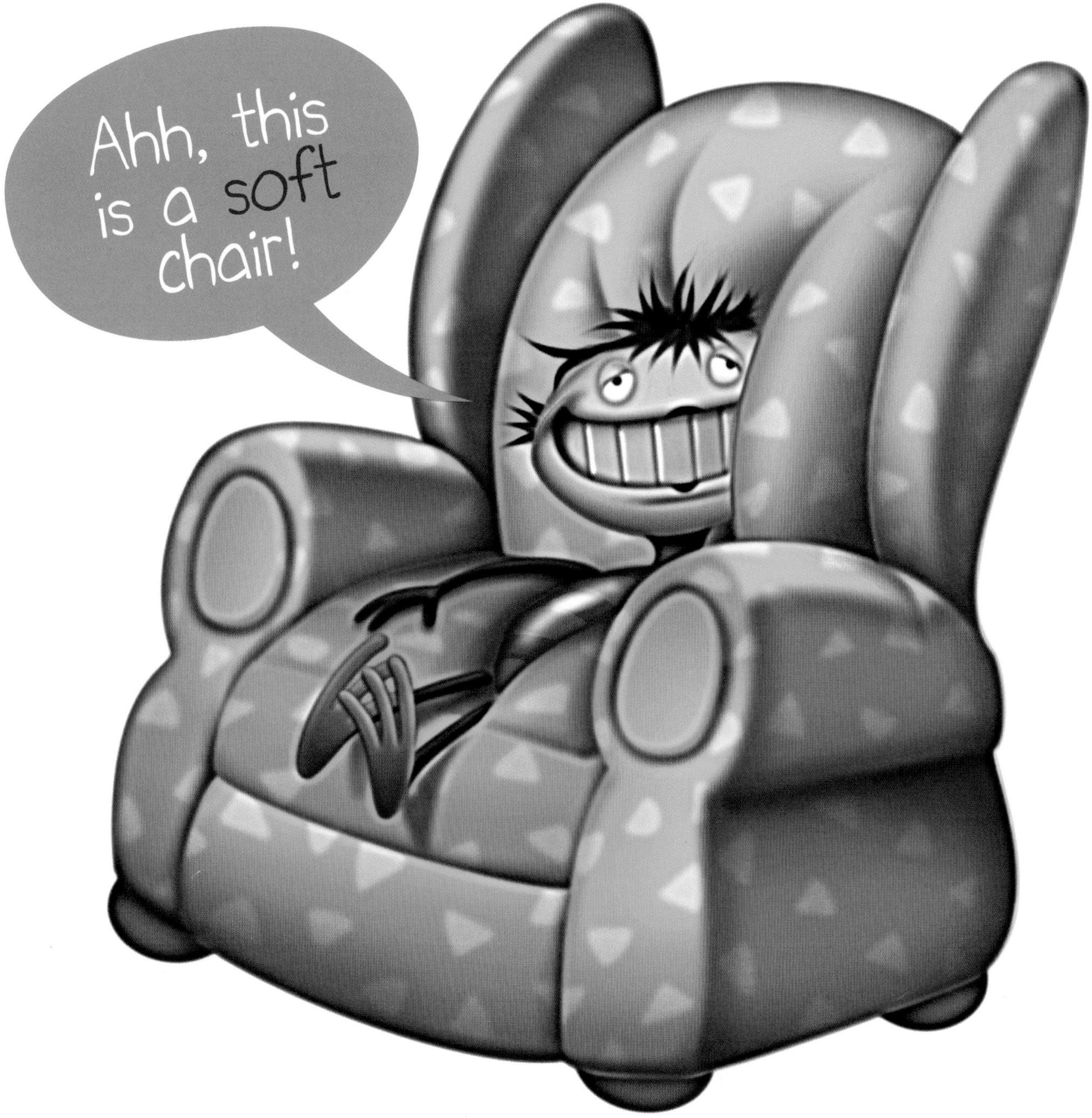
Ahh, this is a soft chair!

Adjective Endings

How can you tell if a word is an adjective? One way is to look at how it ends.

Some adjectives end in *y*.

squeaky   empty   chilly

Some have special endings, such as *able*, *al*, *ful*, *ive*, *less*, and *ous*.

logical   lovable   careless

careful   attractive   dangerous

9

Before and After

Where is the adjective? Usually, it's right before the word it describes.

The tiny dogs bark at the big cats.

Sometimes the adjective comes at the end of a sentence.

These dogs are tiny.

Either way, we know those dogs are small! How do we know? The adjective tells us.

Big, Bigger, and Biggest

You can use adjectives to **compare** things.

If you have two dogs, one is probably bigger. If two cars zoom by, one is probably faster. Some adjectives add *er* to make **comparisons**.

I am faster!

If you ate two desserts yesterday, one was probably more delicious! The other dessert was less delicious. Some adjectives don't sound right with *er*. You wouldn't say "deliciouser." Instead, use more or less.

This is definitely more delicious!

You might think skating is less dangerous than skateboarding. Notice how than can also be used to compare two things.

These cookies are more delicious than that cake.

When two things are equal or the same, use as.

Julian is as smart as Ally.

My cat is not as scary as your dog.

15

Erin is tall, and Jake is taller, but Alexis is the tallest of all. Maybe you've met the fluffiest kitty or the funniest clown.

tallest

fluffiest

funniest

Adjectives that end in *est* compare three or more things.

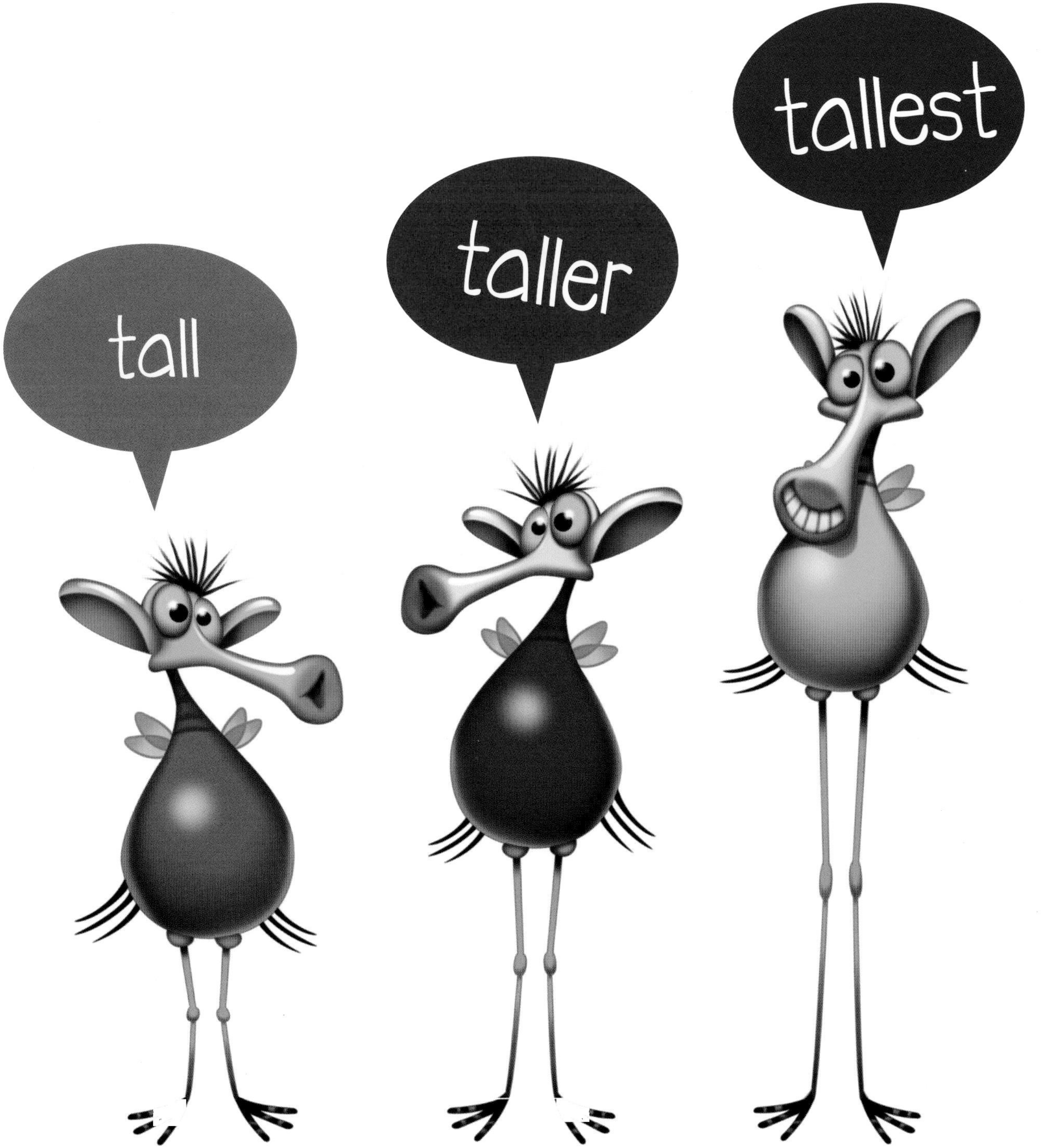
tall
taller
tallest

But some adjectives just don't sound right if you add *est*. You wouldn't say "That was the difficultest test." Or, "These are the uncomfortablest shoes." Instead you'd use most or least.

That was the most difficult test.

These are the least comfortable shoes.

Watch Out!

Don't use an *er* or *est* word with most or least. Choose one way to go! You would never say "more bigger" or "most longest."

Whose Is It?

I hear a bird's song.

The word bird's is an adjective. It shows to whom the song belongs.

This bird's song is beautiful!

I like Ella's idea.   That is the teacher's book.

Have fun at Toby's house!

Ella's, teacher's, and Toby's are more adjectives that show things belong together. You can often spot these adjectives right away. They have an **apostrophe** ('). To make these adjectives, just add an apostrophe and an *s*.

If the word is already **plural**, just add the apostrophe.

I gathered the chickens' eggs.

Hot or Cold?

Opposite adjectives can be lots of fun.

My favorite music is quiet. Your favorite music is loud.

My best friend is short. Your best friend is tall.

What other opposite adjectives can you think up?

I like hot soup.

I like cold soup.

How to Learn More

AT THE LIBRARY

Cleary, Brian P., and Jenya Prosmitsky (illustrator). *Hairy, Scary, Ordinary: What Is an Adjective?* Minneapolis, MN: Carolrhoda, 2000.

Fisher, Doris. *Bowling Alley Adjectives*. Pleasantville, NY: Gareth Stevens, 2008.

Fleming, Maria. *The Bug Book (Adjectives)*. New York: Scholastic, 2004.

McClarnon, Marciann. *Painless Junior Grammar*. Hauppauge, NY: Barron's Educational Series, 2007.

Reeg, Cynthia. *Hamster Holidays: Noun and Adjective Adventures*. St. Louis, MO: Guardian Publishing, 2009.

Schoolhouse Rock: Grammar Classroom Edition. Dir. Tom Warburton. Interactive DVD. Walt Disney, 2007.

ON THE WEB

Visit our home page for lots of links about grammar: *childsworld.com/links*

NOTE TO PARENTS, TEACHERS AND LIBRARIANS: We routinely check our Web links to make sure they're safe, active sites—so encourage your readers to check them out!

Glossary

adjectives (AJ-ik-tivs): Words that describe people, places, things, or ideas. *Sweet* and *beautiful* are adjectives.

apostrophe (uh-POSS-truh-fee): A punctuation mark that shows to what or whom something belongs. The apostrophe in *Ella's cat* shows the cat belongs to Ella.

compare (kum-PAIR): To notice what is the same and what is different between two or more things. Some adjectives help compare two or more things.

comparisons (kum-PAIR-i-suns): Comparisons are when you show how things are the same or different. *Bigger*, *faster*, and *slower* are comparison words.

opposite (OP-uh-zit): Completely different. *Day* and *night* are opposites.

plural (PLOOR-uhl): A word is plural if it names more than one thing. *Monsters* and *cookies* are plural.

Index

24